T H E   L A B Y R I N T H
A N D   T H E
E N N E A G R A M

C I R C L I N G   I N T O   P R A Y E R

JILL KIMBERLY HARTWELL GEOFFRION

AND

ELIZABETH CATHERINE NAGEL

The Pilgrim Press   Cleveland

The Pilgrim Press, 700 Prospect Avenue, Cleveland, Ohio 44115-1100
pilgrimpress.com

© 2001 Jill Kimberly Hartwell Geoffrion and Elizabeth Catherine Nagel

Biblical quotations, unless otherwise noted, are from the New Revised Standard
Version of the Bible, © 1989 by the Division of Christian Education of the
National Council of the Churches of Christ in the U.S.A., and are used by
permission. Alterations have been made to make passages more inclusive.

Printed in the United States of America on acid-free paper

06   05   04   03   02   01   5   4   3   2   1

Library of Congress Cataloging-in-Publication Data

Geoffrion, Jill Kimberly Hartwell, 1958–
     The labyrinth and the enneagram : circling into prayer / Jill Kimberly
Hartwell Geoffrion and Elizabeth Catherine Nagel.
        p.   cm.
     Includes bibliographical references.
     ISBN 0-8298-1450-7
     1. Spiritual life—Christianity.   2. Labyrinths—Religious aspects—
Christianity.   3. Enneagram.   4. Spiritual exercises.   I. Nagel, Elizabeth
Catherine, 1940–   II. Title.

BV4509.5.G46   2001
248—dc21

                                                              2001036830

THE LABYRINTH AND THE ENNEAGRAM

C o n t e n t s

With gratitude to God,
whose creativity fuels ours,
Wisdom Ways Spirituality Center
and Mary Kaye Medinger, its director,
who provided us with the space and opportunity
to develop the seeds of this work,
the monthly retreatants who breathed life
into many of the exercises and experiences
recorded here, and
Madeleine Sue Martin,
whose spiritual visions live on in us.

Diagram of Chartres labyrinth as drawn by Robert Ferré

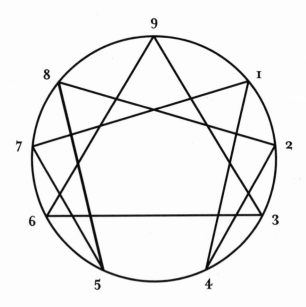

Diagram of Enneagram Circle with Numbers

1 / An Invitation

Let an image of a labyrinth similar to the one on the facing page flow through your mind. Shift your attention to the Enneagram diagram below it. Note its shape. Two circles, two spiritual tools. Now consider the two images together. What do you see?

This book invites you to circle more deeply into prayer. As you use it you will discover much that is not apparent at first glance. We offer to you this ripening fruit of our prayers. May your life be richer, your knowledge of the Holy deeper, and your expressions of your spirituality more fragrant as you explore intersections of these circles.

HOW TO USE THIS BOOK

This book is designed for those who have no prior experience or knowledge of the labyrinth or the Enneagram, as well as those who have spent considerable time with one or both of these spiritual tools.

Each chapter brings into focus one of the nine Enneagram positions of attention. You may work your way through the book from front to back, or you may choose to explore the chapters one by one in any order that appeals. Complete one chapter at a time.

You may use this book in many ways:

- By yourself or with a group that meets together regularly
- As the primary resource for an extended retreat
- Slowly, one labyrinth experience or exercise at a time
- For discovering new approaches to labyrinth praying
- While walking the labyrinth or while using a labyrinth pattern you can trace with your fingers or eyes

Journal pages are provided to record your written and symbolic explorations. Many find it helpful to document their labyrinth experiences through writing, drawing, or composing. Art supplies such as crayons, markers, colored pencils, inexpensive pastels, and paints will support your experiences in meaningful and fun ways. Use them freely whenever you desire.

BASIC LABYRINTH INFORMATION

The labyrinth is a place where we discover in new ways how God is present with us as we walk through life.

Labyrinths are

- Patterns designed to take one to the center—the center of the design, the center of oneself, and the Center of All

- Ancient tools found on every inhabited continent
- Pathways of prayer
- Fields of energy
- Playgrounds
- Mathematical patterns designed to silently reveal deep spiritual and theological truths
- Mirrors of one's interior life
- Transformative spaces for spiritual exploration

Labyrinths are not mazes. Mazes are created to pit the walker against the designer. Labyrinths are winding paths that lead to and from a center without side paths or dead ends.

How does one walk a labyrinth?

- Any way one feels drawn
- As exploration led by one's intuition, thoughts, and heart
- Not always the same way
- Attentively, using what one notices, both internally and externally
- Openly!

What do people report after walking a labyrinth?

- Feeling calmed, centered, and connected
- Noticing what was not evident
- Synchronizing of body, breath, and imagination
- Truth emerging from the inside out

Helpful Hints

Walking the labyrinth begins before you actually enter it. Since the labyrinth is a single path leading to the center, the decision one makes is never "Which way do I go?" but "Am I going to walk it?"

The labyrinth can be used in many ways. It is worth taking time before you start to collect your thoughts and intentions. As you stand at the threshold, pause to focus and pray. How are you going to use this labyrinth walk? Will it be as a time for discovery where you enter with openness and accept what comes? Do you want to use it to pray for someone or some-thing that is very much on your mind and heart? Maybe you wish to pose a question and let your walk be a time for living into the question. Follow what flows from your preparation.

Once you are ready, you may wish to make some gesture or motion. Some people bow. Others cross themselves. Some take a deep breath. Do whatever feels natural. Pray in the way you usually pray.

Now it is time to cross the threshold.

Once you are on the pathway all you have to do is follow it!

Sometimes people want to know, "What happens if I get turned around?" If you are going to the center and get turned around, then you will end up back where you began. If you are leaving the center and get turned around, then you will end up back in the center. It's up to you to choose where to go from where you find yourself. You may decide that your labyrinth experience is complete. Or, you may choose to explore the labyrinth further.

Pay attention to your body and find your pace. It will be different every time you explore the labyrinth. You may find yourself walking very slowly or very quickly. If you are becoming dizzy or getting off balance, then you may need to speed up, slow down, or find a point in the distance for focus.

When walking the labyrinth with others, it's all right to pass another person or to step off the path to let someone go by. Do what feels natural.

In time you will arrive in the center. Your body will have relaxed into its own rhythm and the turnings of the labyrinth will have helped both sides of your brain to become active. Many of the concerns you have brought with you will have fallen away. If there was ever a place of Divine Union, then the center is it. Take time to enjoy the fruit of your prayer! Stand, sit, kneel, or do whatever comes. As a form of embodied prayer, use your body in whatever ways feel natural. Stay as long as feels right. When ready to leave, take the pathway that brought you.

When you get close to the end of the pathway, you may think the experience is almost over. But labyrinth experiences continue to unfold for months. So your experience goes with you. You can't be sure of all its meanings; that's okay. If nothing seemed to happen, then remain open to the possibility that meaning will unfold over time. Be open to ways in which your embodied explorations influence you as you continue to live your life.

The labyrinth can be used in many ways for your explorations. Staying on the path from beginning to end is only one approach. You may follow the path to and from the center. Or you may walk around the labyrinth before, after, or in between labyrinth walks as a way of being with the labyrinth in a different way. Perhaps you will sit by the labyrinth and witness others as they walk. You may want to trace the labyrinth pattern with your finger. You may journal or express yourself in some artistic ways before, after, or during your time walking the labyrinth. As you become more familiar with the labyrinth you may want to start in different places or use only a part of the labyrinth.

We assume you will use a labyrinth in any way that is helpful. All the exercises in this book are meant to help you claim the validity and authority of your own experience. The starting place is where you are now, not where you wish you were, or where you think you are supposed to be.

BASIC ENNEAGRAM INFORMATION

The Enneagram is a tool for understanding ourselves, which is a first step in spiritual growth and transformation.

What is the Enneagram?

- A body of knowledge handed down orally over many centuries
- A dynamic system for understanding our giftedness and our brokenness
- A modern approach drawn from ancient wisdom traditions
- A source for personal illumination
- A tool for examining relationships among different personality types
- A way of understanding how we organize our perceptions
- A system describing nine positions of attention
- A sacred dance calling us to the roots of our spiritual and emotional imbalance
- A road map to the soul

Often the Enneagram is used to determine personality types to deepen self-understanding. Such typing may be done through an oral interview with a person trained in the Enneagram's use. This interview might be done in a group setting or privately with a psychotherapist or spiritual director. Another method is with paper-and-pencil tests, which may be found in some of the books published about the Enneagram or done under the guidance of a person trained to interpret the results. Sometimes a person easily identifies with the characteristics of a certain type. Other persons discover more slowly which type describes them the best.

After we know our type, we begin learning how our particular characteristics are interrelated with other types around the circle. One of the values of this approach to understanding ourselves is that the Enneagram is not about categorizing people.

The Enneagram can be used in another way. Although each of us spends most of our time perceiving the world through one of the nine types, we also have some of the characteristics of each type within us. We are all loyal sometimes. We are all compassionate at other times.

On the pages that follow you do not need to know which Enneagram type describes your way of perceiving. Instead, each chapter invites you to take on characteristics of one type. With one or two types you might wonder how the exercises could take you to a place that feels so natural. In other chapters, you may find it a strain being asked to enter interior terrain that seems or feels so foreign. As you explore the patterns within yourself, you will discover ways you organize your experiences and how these patterns both protect and conceal your true self.

How does one use the Enneagram to pray?

- Listen for the resonance of the type—or lack of resonance
- Attend to faint traces, contradictions, and strong tendencies
- Hold each type as a holy encounter
- Follow your attention to openings into your interior

What do people discover when praying with the Enneagram?

- Defenses that hide their vulnerability and goodness and brokenness

- Courage to confront interior fears, experiences of pain, and self-defeating patterns
- Invitations to move beyond self-protection into healthy vulnerability
- Affirmation of gifts and potential
- Self-understanding
- Transformation!

2 / PERCEIVING MY NEEDS

TWO ENERGY

The words of the ancient psalm
dance through me,
beside green pastures and still waters,
refreshing words of longing,
for I am so weary.

But then the competing voices chime in,
engrained so deep upon my heart.
Be helpful they say, give freely of myself,
put the needs of others first.

Just for once I ask,
how is my soul to be restored?
Who is there for me?

2

ENNEAGRAM TYPE TWO

is characterized by a generous heart and a desire to be helpful to others. Friendships and family are important. Energy is directed to being needed by others and to providing care for people in need. Validation comes through a willingness to respond to the needs of others and the satisfaction received through the affirmation of others. In the willingness to care for others, self-care may be difficult or nonexistent.

AS I BEGIN . . .

Help me
to perceive
what I need.

LABYRINTH EXPERIENCE

Use the labyrinth in this way:
On the way in to the center, pray for others.
On the way out from the center, pray for yourself.

LABYRINTH JOURNAL

Place: Date:

What was my experience of praying for others
as I made my way to the center?

What was my experience of praying for myself
as I made my way from the center?

Personal Reflection:

Read the following and pay attention to where you go in your mind, heart, and body.

It is good that the world has people who care for others. Such altruism, however, does have a negative side. When filling the needs of others becomes your primary need, you may lose, or never develop, the capacity to name your own needs.

When your needs remain unconscious and unclaimed, you fill them indirectly—by becoming manipulative and possessive of others. Friendships are lopsided—you do most of the giving and, in turn, may be manipulated by your friends. You have trouble saying, "No," and want to please others. You want to be important, liked, flattered, and thanked. You might even take on sainthood and martyrdom! In the end, you lose yourself in others by your identification with them.

Spiritually, you may have become convinced that God needs you, rather than that you need God. Driven to be helpful, you may prioritize action and spend little time reflecting. Being alone in a room with nothing to do is likely to make you uncomfortable. The distraction of having someone else to help can keep you at a safe distance from your own interior.

Alone in the presence of the Holy means being face to face with your own neediness. It is there that you see yourself for who you are. It is hard to acknowledge the pride lying underneath your exterior generosity to others and to admit that your giving may be compulsive.

Listening to your own feelings, rather than exercising your highly developed capacity to sense the feelings of others, will help you discover your own value. You find that friendships can be built on mutuality, in which you are loved and love in return. You come to know that God loves you for who you are, not for what you do.

Journal Entry

As I attended to my mind, heart, and body, what did I notice?

Where am I being invited to go?

LABYRINTH EXERCISE

Approach a labyrinth.
Find a place that draws you and go there.
In silence, stay at that place in the presence of the Holy.
When you are ready, leave the labyrinth.
Use the journal entry to reflect on your experience.

LABYRINTH JOURNAL

What was my experience?

SCRIPTURAL REFLECTION

Much of scripture invites us to a cycle of giving and receiving. As we are filled with God's abundance, it is natural and delightful to give. Read the following scripture. Listen for biblical wisdom about giving and receiving.

Jeremiah 17:7–8

Blessed are those who trust in God,
whose trust is God.
They shall be like a tree planted by water,
sending out its roots by the stream.
It shall not fear when heat comes,
and its leaves shall stay green;
in the year of drought it is not anxious,
and it does not cease to bear fruit.

Luke 13:10–13

Jesus was teaching in one of the synagogues on the sabbath. And just then there appeared a woman with a spirit that had crippled her for eighteen years. She was bent over and was quite unable to stand up straight. When Jesus saw her, Jesus called her over and said, "Woman, you are set free from your ailment." When Jesus laid his hands on her, immediately she stood up straight and began praising God.

Psalm 23:1–6

God is my shepherd, I shall not want;
God makes me lie down in green pastures.
God leads me beside still waters;
God restores my soul.
God leads me in right paths
for God's name's sake.
Even though I walk through the darkest valley,
I fear no evil;
for you are with me;

your rod and your staff—
they comfort me.
You prepare a table before me
in the presence of my enemies;
you anoint my head with oil;
my cup overflows.
Surely goodness and mercy shall follow me
all the days of my life;
and I shall dwell in the house of God
my whole life long.

2 Corinthians 1:3–4

Blessed be the . . . God of mercies and the God of all consolation, who consoles us in all our affliction, so that we may be able to console those who are in any affliction with the consolation with which we ourselves are consoled by God.

LABYRINTH EXPERIENCE

With your mind and heart full of these Scriptures you are invited to use the labyrinth to explore the question, "What do I need?"

LABYRINTH JOURNAL

Place: Date:

Gleanings from my labyrinth experience with the question,
"What do I need?"

AS I MOVE ON . . .

Be with me in my walking.
Be with me in my listening.
Open my heart, mind, and body
to receive.

3 / RELEASING MY INNER CRITIC

ONE ENERGY

Sometimes when I least expect it,
the desire for perfection creeps up on me.
At such times, up go my efforts
to get things just right.
Until to my chagrin I find
I've become more driven
to do things well.

It is my ideals
that spur me onward,
believing in this vision of a world
good and true and moral.
Then why, when I work so hard,
does God's peace and joy
elude me so?

ENNEAGRAM TYPE ONE

is characterized by being principled, good, and self-controlled. Responsibility, idealism, and concern for improvement are important. Energy is directed to making a difference in the world, even at great personal sacrifice. Validation comes through such dedication and by getting things done and done right. High expectations, striving for perfection, and adherence to internal standards that are never met lead to chronic irritation and anger that lives just under the surface.

AS I BEGIN . . .

May I know
pleasure,
joy,
relaxation,
happiness,
and love.

FOCUSING

The Gospel of Matthew offers a beautiful story of divine delight. "The heavens were opened . . . and Jesus saw the Spirit of God descending like a dove and alighting on him. And a voice from heaven said, 'This is my Son, the Beloved, with whom I am well pleased.'" (3:16b–17)

You are invited to say aloud, "I am (*your name*)."

Use your imagination to hear God respond, "You, (*your name*), are my beloved; with you I am well pleased."

INVITATION TO GET IN TOUCH WITH YOUR INNER CRITIC

You are invited to pay attention to your gut.

Tell your feelings and thoughts to be quiet.

What is the first thing that comes to mind when you hear:

I should . . .

I didn't . . .

I ought to have . . .

When things don't go well, I . . .

I never . . .

My greatest critic is . . .

I'm lacking in . . .

When something is out of place, I . . .

I feel guilty when . . .

When someone questions my value, I . . .

I have failed to . . .

Being out of control is . . .

JOURNAL ENTRY

Remaining alert to your experience of your gut, reflect silently on these questions:

What has this experience generated inside?

What happens to me when I make these kinds of statements to myself?

What is it like when I have a bad day that lasts all week?
What does and doesn't get done?

What is it like when my inner critic gets going full tilt?

What good comes out of the experiences of my inner critic talking to me?

LABYRINTH EXPERIENCE

Stay with your gut and its truths as you go to a labyrinth. Follow the path in and out without stopping, even in the center. Stay alert to what is going on inside.

LABYRINTH JOURNAL

Place: Date:

What communications did I receive from my gut?

APPROACHING LABYRINTHS

The labyrinth is a wonderful place to experiment with letting go! Some different kinds of letting go are forgiveness, willingness to try something new, releasing a long-term habit, changing your mind, or ignoring others' expectations.

One of the beauties of the labyrinth is that it is a safe place to open yourself to your own experience. Here you can allow yourself to be drawn in to what is happening rather than having to shape or control it.

Let go of all your expectations as you move towards the labyrinth— except the one that something will happen—even though you will have no idea what it will be. Say to yourself, "I don't need to be responsible for what happens here." Resist any attempt to figure out what might happen on the labyrinth!

Pay close attention to spontaneous experiences of joy or pleasure that come on the labyrinth—especially today!

If you get an urge to play while on the labyrinth—play!

You can skip.

You can roll.

You can experiment and find out what happens if you follow the lines instead of the path.

You can ask the question, "What would I do if no one was looking?" Do it if you want!

LABYRINTH EXPERIENCE

IMAGINE! Imagine that all is as it should be. You don't have to believe that all is as it should be. For this small slice of time commit yourself to an act of imagination.

Enter a labyrinth. As you are moving, if anything—a thought, a feeling, a memory, a gut reaction—contradicts that all is as it should be, acknowledge it by physically stopping where you are. If you find yourself resisting doing this, then notice and acknowledge it. Then try to move into your imagination!

As contradictions come, let them go. Let them go mentally, or let them go physically. Symbolically shake them away, push them away, drop them—whatever you need to do to get rid of them!

Once you have let go, begin moving on the labyrinth again, imagining that all is as it should be.

Feel free to stop as many times as you need. If that means every step, do it!

When you get to the center you have full permission to acknowledge and experience joy and pleasure.

LABYRINTH JOURNAL

Place: Date:

My experience of this labyrinth walk was . . .

From stopping and restarting I learned . . .

Attentiveness to pleasure or joy coming from within helped me perceive . . .

AS I MOVE ON . . .

You are invited to say aloud, "I am (*your name*)."

Use your imagination to hear God respond, "You, (*your name*), are my beloved; with you I am well pleased."

Be with me in my walking.
Be with me in my listening.
Open my heart, mind, and body
to receive.

4 / Moving Towards Freedom

Six Energy

It would seem belonging
would be its own reward,
security derived
from the covenant of friends to stand together,
the assurance of community
in a world so focused on individualism.

Surely others will honor
commitments given one other,
each person valuing, as I do,
qualities of faithfulness and loyalty.

Why then do I fear?

ENNEAGRAM TYPE SIX

is characterized by loyalty to both friends and beliefs, manifested through allegiance with like-minded people. Energy is directed to defending family and community and to vigilance in an unsafe world. Validation comes from establishing relationships of trust and being faithful. Underlying this stalwart devotion to others is a fear of not being able to survive alone or of being abandoned.

AS I BEGIN . . .

May I trust.

LABYRINTH EXPERIENCE

Searching your memory, jot down ten situations in which you feel faithful and loyal or you have a sense of belonging.

Now you are invited to walk the labyrinth holding these situations in your mind.

LABYRINTH JOURNAL

Place: Date:

What did I discover on the labyrinth about my faithfulness and loyalty?

What did I discover about belonging?

LABYRINTH EXPERIENCE

Name your fears out loud. Choose one.
Write it down.

Exaggerate your fear to the point where it becomes ludicrous.
Describe your fear now.

Go to a labyrinth.
Talk with this fear as you move on the labyrinth.

LABYRINTH JOURNAL

Place: Date:

Locate your box of crayons, markers, or colored pencils.
A representation of my discoveries:

GAINING FOCUS: EXERCISE

When would you describe yourself with the following nouns or adjectives? Let the words float around and through you, evoking images of yourself in various places and with various people. Observe your thoughts.

COOPERATIVE	GOOD SPORT
REALISTIC	RELIABLE
WARM-HEARTED	RESPECTFUL
DEFIANT	DEPENDENT
LOYAL	CAUTIOUS
INTUITIVE	VIGILANT
GOOD PLANNER	PROCRASTINATOR
AUTHORITARIAN	BIG RISK TAKER
TEAM PLAYER	TRADITIONAL
OBEDIENT	ANXIOUS
RESPONSIBLE	SUSPICIOUS
FAIR	TRUTHTELLER

Consider the following questions.
When do you look to others for authority?

When does security become your number-one priority?
When do you play it safe?

When are you tempted to view things as only right and wrong?

When are you on guard?

When do you look for others to set the limits?

When do you desire clear boundaries?

When do you do really risky things?

LABYRINTH EXPERIENCE

Find a place of safety inside yourself. Once you have located it and feel secure, bring to mind a difficult area of your life where you feel at odds. Use the labyrinth to explore this area. Listen to those parts of yourself that are faithful, loyal, and willing to let go of fears. Trust God to be your companion.

LABYRINTH JOURNAL

Place: Date:

What happened?

AS I MOVE ON . . .

Be with me in my walking.
Be with me in my listening.
Open my heart, mind, and body
to receive.

5 / FROM GRIEF TO GRACE

FOUR ENERGY

Like prayer beads upon a string
I count my losses.
How did life ever get to be so hard?
If I were in charge of writing my life story,
I'd make some major changes.

Where in all of this I ask, is meaning?
Something of value, a glimpse of beauty?
Surely I've not suffered
All this grief and pain for nothing.

4

Enneagram Type Four

is characterized by sensitivity to feelings, intensity, and creative drive. Searching for the unique and the original are important. Energy is directed to exploring the pain and suffering in themselves and others. Validation comes from being able to translate this exploration into universal understandings of loss and spiritual reality. In this search to understand the significance of personal experience, there is the risk of withdrawing, becoming self-absorbed, and resisting change.

AS I BEGIN . . .

May I grieve well
that I might live well
and give well.

CREATING AN ENVIRONMENT

Make sure your art supplies are available.

If possible, choose some favorite music to play while you are walking the labyrinth.

Look around you. Find ordinary things that have meaning for you. These could include a stone, book, pen, mug, scarf, or piece of fabric. If possible, locate a candle and some matches.

Arrange these in a way that is beautiful to you. Light the candle.

Return to this environment whenever you finish walking the labyrinth.

BECOMING READY

Get comfortable. Allow the beauty of your environment to feed your spirit. Sense your heart. Allow it to open. Invite yourself to support its many expressions.

When you feel ready, move to the labyrinth.

LABYRINTH EXPERIENCE

Walk the labyrinth sensing your heart.

LABYRINTH JOURNAL

Place: Date:

Use your art supplies to record the expressions of your heart.

Imagine . . .

Imagine a story in which you are the central character. Make sure to include elements of loss and abandonment. Feel no obligation to create a "happy" ending.

Outline your story below.

Consider times in your life that mirror the story you just created. Write or draw about them.

LABYRINTH EXPERIENCE

Remember a time when you were abandoned.
Mourn your loss as you walk to the center.
In the center choose to set aside your grief.
As you walk out, bring to heart those who love and support you.

LABYRINTH JOURNAL

Place: Date:

Without picking your pen up from the paper draw what you are feeling.

LABYRINTH EXPERIENCE

Look at your drawing.

Use the labyrinth as a dance floor to further explore what you are discovering.

LABYRINTH JOURNAL

Place: Date:

I am discovering . . .

Out of these experiences, what do I have to share with the rest of the world?

AS I MOVE ON . . .

Pick up each object you collected.
Bless it.
Return it to its place.

Be with me in my walking.
Be with me in my listening.
Open my heart, mind, and body
to receive.

Blow out your candle.

6 / LAYING CLAIM AND TAKING ACTION

NINE ENERGY

In a world so filled with conflict,
is it not better to find the path
that angers none?
To mediate and reconcile?
For how can harmony and peace be faulted?

Yet as I listen carefully to others
as a way to determine
who I might be
a damp malaise settles in,
until I discover
I am stuck and going nowhere,
my soul stalled out in neutral.

9

ENNEAGRAM TYPE NINE

is characterized by the search for harmony and peace. Attentiveness to others and giving support are important. Energy is directed to peace-making and seeing the points of view of others. Validation comes from belonging, acceptance by others, and responsiveness to others' agendas. With this desire to go along with others comes avoidance of conflict, in-decision, and the loss of identity.

AS I BEGIN . . .

May my energy
fuel my willingness to commit.

LABYRINTH EXPERIENCE

Take this book with you and stand somewhere on the outside of the
labyrinth.

Close your eyes and center yourself in your body.
When you feel grounded, open your eyes.
Be attentive to your experience of this moment.

Read one scripture selection at a time out loud.
When you have finished say to yourself, "I am invited to step into
God's peace."
Then, take one step on the labyrinth towards its center.

For everything there is a season, and a time for every matter under heaven
. . . and a time for peace. (Ecclesiastes 3:1, 8d)
I am invited to step into God's peace.
(Take one step toward the center.)

[Wisdom's] ways are ways of pleasantness,
and all its paths are peace. (Proverbs 3:17)
I am invited to step into God's peace.
(Take one step toward the center.)

Peace I [Jesus] leave with you; my peace I give to you. . . . Do not let your
hearts be troubled, and do not let them be afraid. (John 14:27)
I am invited to step into God's peace.
(Take one step toward the center.)

. . . to set the mind on the Spirit is life and peace. (Romans 8:6b)
I am invited to step into God's peace.
(Take one step toward the center.)

Let us . . . pursue what makes for peace and for mutual upbuilding.
(Romans 14:19)
I am invited to step into God's peace.
(Take one step toward the center.)

Now may the [God] of peace . . . give you peace at all times in all ways.
(2 Thessalonians 3:16a)
I am invited to step into God's peace.
(Take one step toward the center.)

May mercy, peace, and love be yours in abundance. (Jude 1:2)
I am invited to step into God's peace.
(Take one step toward the center.)

LABYRINTH JOURNAL

Place: Date:

As I stepped into God's peace I was choosing to . . .

LABYRINTH EXPERIENCE

For this exercise, complete one step at a time without reading ahead! Trust that the way will unfold.

- Locate six pieces of paper.

- On a piece of paper write your full name. Turn it over and draw a symbol expressing who you are.

- Take a moment to identify five people who are significant in your life. Write one name on each of the five remaining papers.

- Go to the labyrinth carrying the paper with your name and symbol on it. Walk until you find a place that feels like "yours." Be looking for a place that seems like "home"—somewhere that uniquely draws you today, and therefore reflects who you are at this moment. When you get there, pause and enjoy it. If you reach the center without stopping, then pause there.

- Ask yourself, "Where am I?" When you are ready, place your paper on the labyrinth with the symbol showing.

- Leave the labyrinth and return to your five pieces of paper. Quickly place each of your five papers in a different place on the labyrinth. Step off the labyrinth.

- Go to one of the papers without your symbol. Read the name and bring that person's memory to you. Imagine that this is the place that the person would have chosen.

- Begin walking the labyrinth from here. You can walk either direction; it doesn't matter. Continue walking for about five minutes and then leave the labyrinth.

- Following these directions, go to a different paper. Again, bring that person's memory to you and walk from this person's place. Repeat this until you have walked from each of the pieces of paper.

LABYRINTH JOURNAL

Place: Date:

Close your eyes and center yourself. When you are grounded, open your eyes.

When I walked out of another person's place it was like . . .

Reflect on the following questions. You may use words or phrases, explore
with color on paper, or respond through creating sounds.

Where in my life have I:
Allowed other people to tell me who I am and what's expected of me?

Followed someone else's path?

Gone with "the flow" rather than rocking the boat, even though the flow wasn't mine?

Been caught, stuck, or paralyzed in indecision?

LABYRINTH EXPERIENCE

Return to the place on the labyrinth where you put the paper with your name and symbol.

Close your eyes and ground yourself in your space. When you are centered, open your eyes.

Taking into account today's experiences, use the labyrinth to explore: Something you need to do or a direction you need to go.

When finished, write down, on the paper with your name and symbol, an action that you are going to take.

Use the labyrinth to explore the action that you are going to take.

LABYRINTH JOURNAL

Place: Date:

An image of myself doing what I have decided I need to do:

AS I MOVE ON . . .

Hold the paper with your name, symbol, and action you are going to take over the center of your body.

Be with me in my walking.
Be with me in my listening.
Open my heart, mind, and body
to receive.

7 / WISDOM INFORMING KNOWLEDGE

FIVE ENERGY

Hungry to know, I read another book,
ask another question,
soak up more information.
At least I'm not compelled like some
to read cereal boxes.

It is easier to go on collecting knowledge,
losing myself in the grand pursuit
of others' thoughts and work,
so much there is to know.

Except sometimes I wonder why it is
The psalmist's cry is
for wisdom taught in one's secret heart.
Or why wisdom has its beginning
by being awestruck
with the Divine?

5

ENNEAGRAM TYPE FIVE

is characterized by a hunger for knowledge, perceptiveness, and the gifts of being an observer. Both objectivity and privacy of self are important. Energy is directed to wanting to know why the world works as it does and asking questions. Validation comes from time spent alone to recharge and to pursue the quest for understanding. By suspending feelings in the quest for truth, one risks isolation, detachment, and the confusion of knowledge and information with wisdom.

AS I BEGIN . . .

May my knowing
benefit us all.

GETTING STARTED

Take a candle and some matches to a labyrinth.

Identify three places in your life where you are looking for wisdom.

When you have done this, light the candle in honor of your search for wisdom.

LABYRINTH EXPERIENCE

Look at the labyrinth.

Spend at least five minutes noticing everything you can.

LABYRINTH JOURNAL

Place: Date:

I noticed . . .

I also noticed . . ..

And I noticed . . ..

Exploration

The labyrinth engages

  my muscles,

  emotions,

  spirit,

  brain

  and imagination.

What do I need to know about the labyrinth to make greater sense of my bodily experiences of praying it?

My responses:

I Know the Labyrinth As . . .

When a friends asks, "What is a labyrinth?" my experiences will lead me to say . . .

Labryinths are

    single paths which lead to and from a center

    spiritual tools

    ancient symbols

    places of prayer

    significant patterns

Identifying Questions

What are my questions about labyrinths?

Frequently Asked Questions Relating to Labyrinths

Where did labyrinths come from?

No one is certain. The oldest known example is from Greece and has been dated 1200 B.C.E.

Where are labyrinths found?

On every inhabited continent, in countries such as Brazil, the United States, Iceland, Egypt, Sumatra, Norway, Crete, Russia, India, Australia, and South Africa.

Is there one labyrinth pattern or several?

There are many patterns.

How have labyrinths been used?

People use labyrinths according to their differing needs. They have been used as decorations, in myths, ceremonially, and as walking pathways.

What is the first example of Christian use of the labyrinth?

A labyrinth was placed in a church floor mosaic in 324 C.E. in Algiers, North Africa. Other Christian examples in Italy, Spain, and Ireland are based on the seven circuit pattern. The pattern used in this book was laid in the floor of Chartres Cathedral in France around 1200 C.E.

LABYRINTH EXPERIENCE

Pretend you know everything you need to know about labyrinths. Follow the pathway of the labyrinth below with a pen or pencil held in the hand you don't usually use. As you move along the pathway make a small circle to mark a place where you feel safe and an X to mark a place where you don't.

LABYRINTH JOURNAL

Place: Date:

My Xs show me . . .

My small circles show me . . .

LABYRINTH EXPERIENCE

Walk the labyrinth asking:
When do I withdraw?
Where do I detach?
Why do I disconnect?
How do I hide?

LABYRINTH JOURNAL

Place: Date:

I discovered:

AS I MOVE ON . . .

Return to the candle lit in honor of your search for wisdom.
Name the wisdom that you have gleaned while working with the labyrinth.
Blow out your candle with gratitude for the wisdom received.

Be with me in my walking.
Be with me in my listening.
Open my heart, mind, and body
to receive.

THREE ENERGY

Running though my mental laundry list,
I review all those things
I need yet to do.
So much satisfaction derived
when I hit the bed at night,
checking off the many things I've done.
Whatever would others do
without me!

Then why this small gnawing voice inside,
surrounded as I am
by all my grand activity and successes.
This nagging disquiet
which eats away,
by saying
there must be more.

3

ENNEAGRAM TYPE THREE

is characterized by pragmatism, achievement, and the need to get things done. Competing and winning, efficiency, and feeling worthwhile are important. Energy is directed to enthusiastic leadership, which motivates others to develop and be productive. Validation comes from accomplishments, status, and success. The risk comes from the confusion of performance and production with who one is and how one feels.

AS I BEGIN . . .

May I find courage
to be grounded
in my self.

GETTING STARTED

Go to a labyrinth.

Enter and follow the pathway to the center.

As soon as you get there, walk straight out. Do not follow the winding path out.

LABYRINTH JOURNAL

Place: Date:

What did I discover as I walked the labyrinth today?

LABYRINTH EXPERIENCE

Go to a labyrinth.

Enter and follow the pathway to the center.

As soon as you get there, walk straight out. Do not follow the winding path out.

LABYRINTH JOURNAL

Place: Date:

What did I discover as I repeated my experience?

LABYRINTH EXPERIENCE

Walk around the outside of the labyrinth once and notice where you feel drawn to go. As you walk, which part of the labyrinth is most inviting?

Once you have circled the whole labyrinth, make your way to the place that calls you. If you aren't sure, pick a spot and go there.

Get comfortable and rest wherever you are on the labyrinth. Believe something sacred will emerge from within.

Rest for ten minutes. Resist any urges you feel to move. After ten minutes get up and complete the labyrinth journal exercise.

LABYRINTH JOURNAL

Place: Date:

The invitation was to believe that something sacred would emerge from within. Reflect on what you found in your own interior. Use your art supplies.

EXERCISE

How would you describe yourself, when you are acting as the person who gets things done, the do-er? As quickly as possible, write whatever words or phrases come into your consciousness.

Reflections

What is the first thing you notice about what is on your list?

Being productive is a societal ideal. It also has an underside to it. You can get so busy doing things that you get disconnected from feelings, self, and others. It becomes easy to focus on tasks and to neglect relationships.

You can use the labyrinth to interrupt the flow that society cultivates and rewards.

What happened when you walked to the center and then walked out?

What happened when you rested in the place that drew you?

What images emerge out of your experiences?

LABYRINTH EXPERIENCE

Return to the place that drew you. Choose a direction and walk the labyrinth from there.

You may:

Walk to the center and follow the path out.

Walk out and consider that a "complete" walk.

Walk to the exit/entrance. Turn around and walk back in.

Let your heart lead you where you need to go.

LABYRINTH JOURNAL

Place: Date:

Where did your heart lead you?

PAPER LABYRINTH EXERCISE

Use this paper labyrinth as a prayer tool to explore ways in which you can be present in your relationships during the next week. You may include people who are living or dead, who are physically, emotionally, or spiritually present.

You can use the labyrinth image any way you like: gazing at it, writing words on it or across it, tracing the path with your fingers, or coloring it. Let your internal promptings guide you.

Use this paper labyrinth as a prayer tool to explore other ways in which you can be present to yourself in the next week.

Use this paper labyrinth as a prayer tool to further explore ways in which you can be present to God in the next week.

AS YOU MOVE ON . . .

Go directly to the center of the labyrinth. Do not walk the path in.
Walk out, following the path.

Take your experience with you, letting it nurture you in the coming
week.

Be with me in my walking.
Be with me in my listening.
Open my heart, mind, and body
to receive.

9 / SEARCHING FOR TRUTH AND JUSTICE

EIGHT ENERGY

"It's not right," I rage, "Not fair!"
The familiar words leap from my belly,
my passion for justice roused up.
One more time I charge ahead,
confronting what needs changing
or extending protection
to someone oppressed.

Why is it then when the truth,
which is so obvious,
calls for strength and action,
I look around
and find myself alone?

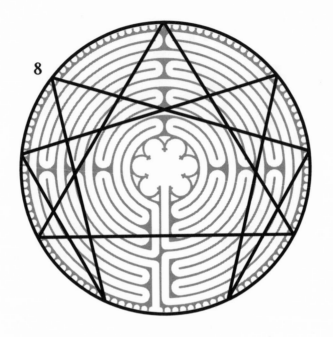

ENNEAGRAM TYPE EIGHT

is characterized by being strong-willed, self-confident, and confrontational. Feeling strong, secure, and courageous is important. Energy is directed to fighting back to resist being controlled by others and to right injustice. Validation comes from being powerful, in control, and through effecting change in the world. When so much energy is focused on confronting the world, the truths about oneself, vulnerability, and emotional connection with others will be elusive.

AS I BEGIN . . .

May I find the grace
to embody my own truth.

GETTING STARTED

Stand in the middle of the room and announce one truth about yourself.
Now write it down.

EXERCISE

Consider: "If I had one billion dollars and could use it any way I wanted to
help make something right, what would I do?"

Notes on what I would do:

Offer a prayer on behalf of those who would benefit from your action.

The labyrinth
is your tool to use
in whatever ways you need.

Spend five minutes putting color on paper
as a way of exploring these statements:

The labyrinth invites you
to learn to use your strengths.

It supports your asserting,
"This is what I need."

It welcomes your questioning,
"What responses are coming back?"

The labyrinth
teaches you to trust
that your experience will lead you to truth.

Often times society
insists it's the other way around,
"This is the Truth;
you are expected
to form your experience
around it."

My explorations of these statements:

LABYRINTH EXPERIENCE

Who needs to be protected? Think about an occasion or situation that has to do with justice that is burning for you right now. Use the labyrinth to explore it.

Feel free to use any approach. You can walk the path, use a section, walk across the labyrinth, sit on it (you can use a chair if you would like), walk on the lines instead of the path, go to the center, or pace back and forth across it . . .

Do whatever you need to focus your energy as you explore an injustice.

LABYRINTH JOURNAL

Place: Date:

What was your burning issue?

What was your experience?

What is your truth?

LABYRINTH EXPERIENCE

Identify a situation in which you felt crushed and wanted to fight back. Even if you didn't act on it, recall how you wanted to push back. Rather than being controlled, you would have liked it better if you had been in control.

Use the labyrinth in any way that is helpful as you explore this situation.

LABYRINTH JOURNAL

Place: Date:

In what situation did you want to fight back?

What was your experience?

What are your truths?

LABYRINTH EXPERIENCE

In what situation would you would like to say what you really feel and think? Imagine being as direct, blunt, and honest as you could possibly be.
Go to the labyrinth and work on it.

LABYRINTH JOURNAL

Place: Date:

The situation about which I wanted to say what I think and feel is . . .

My experience on the labyrinth was . . .

My truths are . . .

Reflection

What happened during the three times of exploration?

What did these experiences draw out of me?

What was unexpected?

Where was I vulnerable?

AS I MOVE ON . . .

Go to the center of the labyrinth. Offer thanks for your truths—truths that came not only from today, but truths that you have become aware of recently.

Be with me in my walking.
Be with me in my listening.
Open my heart, mind, and body
to receive.

10 / THE PAIN AND PLEASURE OF POSSIBILITIES

SEVEN ENERGY

Just as I learned as a child
when I would turn the teacher's voice
into a pleasant background drone,
I again stare out of the window,
letting my mind wander free.

Imagine! All those marvelous things
I could do.
Places to go, fun I could have.
In my mind, I elaborate amazing adventures,
one possibility tumbling after another,
all in technicolor.

With a start I come back to reality.
Reality?
My daydreams are more fun!
So, what is real?

7

ENNEAGRAM TYPE SEVEN

is characterized by spontaneity, a love of new adventures, and enthusiasm. Anticipation of future events and exciting possibilities are important. Energy is directed to making plans, developing contingency options, and creating imaginative projects. Validation comes from the joy and optimism of experiencing life. In this continuous movement of searching for new experiences, other possibilities that could be gained from focusing, staying with something, or making a commitment are lost.

AS I BEGIN . . .

May I embrace the emotions that come,
whether they bring me pleasure
or pain.

GETTING STARTED

Smile broadly. Let out a laugh. Think about one thing you are looking forward to. Express thanks for one recent experience of joy or pleasure.

EXERCISE

How many things that you find pleasurable can you list in five minutes?

LABYRINTH EXPERIENCE

Go to a labyrinth to consider the question, "What do I imagine my future to be?" Use the path creatively. Be sure to include some ways in which you will have fun.

LABYRINTH JOURNAL

Place: Date:

What imaginings did I have?

What were my experiences of joy, fun, and pleasure?

EXERCISE

Document the experiences you have just had with art supplies by cutting out shapes, making a collage, creating a sculpture, composing a song, or any other way you'd like.

LABYRINTH EXPERIENCE

When some people think of the future they are inclined to focus on potential difficulties. Others have so much fun with the images that come to mind that they just keep elaborating. Which of these two ways best describes your inclination?

Now choose one of the two following ways to walk the labyrinth. Pick the option that is most unnatural for you. Do not cheat!

Think of all the obstacles and places
where there might be pain in your future.

Or:

Explore your vision of the future further,
paying particular attention to the positive aspects
and possibilities.

Go to a labyrinth and explore the option you've chosen. Use the labyrinth in any way that you would like.

LABYRINTH JOURNAL

Place: Date:

What did you choose to explore?

Where did your explorations take you?

EXERCISE

If possible, go and find someone to talk to. Share about your labyrinth experiences relating to your future. Enjoy!

AS I MOVE ON . . .

Hear the invitation of the Holy: Move from your imagination
into the reality of your life. Go in joy!

Be with me in my walking.
Be with me in my listening.
Open my heart, mind, and body
to receive.

11 / A Further Invitation

Now that you have walked through these experiences, we invite you to continue your explorations. If some exercises or labyrinth experiences could yield more fruit in your life, then return to them. Our hope is that as you circle more deeply into prayer you will be open to the creativity that is flowing through you.

Blessings on your paths!

RESOURCES

Labyrinth

Artress, Lauren. *Walking a Sacred Path: Rediscovering the Labyrinth as a Spiritual Tool.* New York: Riverhead Books, 1995.

Attali, Jacques. *The Labyrinth in Culture and Society.* Berkeley, CA: North Atlantic Books, 1999.

Campbell, Scott. *Mazes and Labyrinths: A Search for the Center.* Scottsdale, AZ: Lutz Limited, 1996, videocassette.

Champion, Alex B. *Essays on Labyrinths and Other Geometric Symbols.* Philo, CA: Earth Maze Publishing, 1999.

Cousineau, Phil. *The Art of Pilgrimage: The Seeker's Guide to Making Travel Sacred.* Berkeley, CA: Conari Press, 1998.

Curry, Helen. *The Way of the Labyrinth: A Powerful Meditation for Everyday Life.* New York: Penguin Compass, 2000.

Doob, Penelope Reed. *The Idea of the Labyrinth from Classical Antiquity Through the Middle Ages.* Ithaca, NY: Cornell University Press, 1990.

Ferré, Robert. *The Labyrinth Revival.* St. Louis, MO: One Way Press, 1996.

———. *The Origin of the Chartres Labyrinth Pattern.* St. Louis, MO: One Way Press, 1999.

Geoffrion, Jill Kimberly Hartwell. *Praying the Labyrinth: A Journal for Spiritual Creativity.* Cleveland, OH: Pilgrim Press, 1999.

———. *Living the Labyrinth: 101 Paths to a Deeper Connection with the Sacred.* Cleveland, OH: Pilgrim Press, 2000.

Haskolski, Helmut. *The Labyrinth: Symbol of Fear, Rebirth and Liberation.* Translated by Michael H. Kohn. Boston: Shambhala, 1997.

Kidd, Sue Monk. "A Guiding Feminine Myth." In *The Dance of the Dissident Daughter,* 107–130. San Francisco: HarperSanFrancisco, 1996.

Labyrinths: Their Mystery and Magic. Staatsburg, NY: Penny Price Media, 1997, videocasssette.

Lonegren, Sig. *Labyrinths: Ancient Myths and Modern Uses.* Glastonbury: Gothic Image Publications, 1996.

McMillen, Joan. *Remembering the Way: Ceremony in Honor of the Labyrinth at Chartres.* Menlo Park, CA: Joan Marie McMillen, 1989, audiocassette.

O'Roark, Mary Ann. "A Walk Through Time." *Guideposts* 54 (7 September, 1999): 40–43.

Pennick, Nigel. *Mazes and Labyrinths.* London: Robert Hale, 1990.

Sands, Helen Raphael. *The Healing Labyrinth: Finding Your Path to Inner Peace.* New York: Barrons, 2001.

Saward, Jeff. *Ancient Labyrinths of the World.* Thundersley, England: Caerdroia, 1997.

Schaper, Donna and Carole Ann Camp. *Labyrinths from the Outside In.* Woodstock, VT: Skylight Paths Publishing, 2000.

Villette, Jean. *The Enigma of the Labyrinth.* Translated by Robert Ferré and Ruth Hanna. St. Louis, MO: One Way Press, 1995.

West, Melissa Gayle. *Exploring the Labyrinth: A Guide for Healing and Spiritual Growth.* NY: Broadway Books, 2000.

Enneagram

Bane, Roseanne. *Dancing in the Dragon's Den: Rekindling the Creative Fire in Your Shadow.* York Beach, ME: Nicholas-Hay, distributed by Samuel Weiser, Inc., 1999.

Baren, Renee, and Elizabeth Wagele. *The Enneagram Made Easy: Discover the 9 Types of People.* San Francisco: HarperSanFrancisco, 1994.

Daniels, David N., and Virginia A. Price. *The Essential Enneagram: The Definitive Personality Test and Self-Discovery Guide.* San Francisco: HarperSanFrancisco, 2000.

Maitri, Sandra. *The Spiritual Dimensions of the Enneagram: Nine Faces of the Soul.* New York: The Putman Publishing Group, 2001.

Metz, Barbara, and John Burchill. *The Enneagram and Prayer: Discovering Our True Selves Before God.* Denville, NJ: Dimension Books, Inc., 1987.

Mortz, Mary E. *Overcoming our Compulsions: Using the Twelve Steps and the Enneagram as Spiritual Tools for Life.* Liguori, MO: Liguori Publications, 1994.

Palmer, Helen. *The Enneagram: Understanding Yourself and the Others in Your Life.* Cambridge: Harper and Row, 1988.

———. *The Enneagram in Love and Work.* San Francisco: HarperSanFrancisco, 1995.

———. *The Enneagram Workshop.* Boulder, CO: Sounds True Recordings, 1991, audiocassette.

———. *The Pocket Enneagram: Understanding the 9 Types of People.* San Francisco: HarperSanFrancisco, 1995.

———. *The Enneagram Advantage.* New York: Harmony Books, 1998.

Riso, Don Richard. *Personality Types: Using the Enneagram for Self-Discovery.* Boston: Houghton Mifflin Co., 1987.

Riso, Don Richard, and Russ Hudson. *The Wisdom of the Enneagram: The Complete Guide to Psychological and Spiritual Growth for the Nine Personality Types.* New York: Bantam Books, 1999.

Rohr, Richard, and Andreas Ebert. *Discovering the Enneagram: An Ancient Tool for a New Spiritual Journey.* Translated by Peter Heinegg. New York: Crossroads, 1990.

_____. *Experiencing the Enneagram.* New York: Crossroads, 1992.

White, Erin. "Labyrinth." *Sacred Journey* (August 2000): 35–43.

Zuercher, Suzanne. *Enneagram Spirituality: From Compulsion to Contemplation.* Notre Dame: Ave Maria Press, 1992, audiocassette.

_____. *The Enneagram, Personality and Prayer: Using the Enneagram to Enrich Your Spiritual Life.* Notre Dame: Ave Maria Press, 1993, audiocassette.

Other Books from The Pilgrim Press

SACRED JOURNEY
Spiritual Wisdom for Times of Transition
MIKE RIDDELL

This inspiring and challenging book is for anyone who has ever asked, "What now?" or "What will be left of my life when I'm gone?" Storyteller and writer Mike Riddell puts his finger on the malaise that can overtake us at times during our lives and shows us how to make it an opportunity for refocusing on what really matters.

0-8298-1456-6/224 pages/paper/$16.00

LIKE A SECOND LAYER OF SKIN
100 Affirmations for Faithful Living
DOROTHY WINBUSH RILEY

These affirmations empower readers to live their lives to the fullest. Each is a poetic statement, and together they affirm faith, prayer life, love of self, love for others, and love of God. Reading these aloud gives an opportunity to create the kind of spiritual environment in which we would want to live.

0-8298-1411-6/112 pages/paper/$10.00

DEEP IN THE FAMILIAR
Four Life Rhythms
JOAN CANNON BORTON

This book reinterprets the four traditional Hindu life phases into four life rhythms for women viewed through the Christian experience. These rhythms are "Student" or learner; "Householder" or family and community member; "Time in the forest," which names the need for solitude; and "The return to the village," a woman's place of connection and authenticity.

0-8298-1408-6/208 pages/paper/$16.00

PRAYING THE LABYRINTH
A Journal for Spiritual Exploration

JILL KIMBERLY HARTWELL GEOFFRION

This book is a journal that leads readers into spiritual exercise of self-discovery through scripture selections, journaling questions, and poetry, with generous space for personal reflections.

0-8298-1343-8/128 pages/paper/$12.95

LIVING THE LABYRINTH
101 Paths to a Deeper Connection with the Sacred

JILL KIMBERLY HARTWELL GEOFFRION

This book offers beginners and seasoned labyrinth users a multitude of new ways to approach this sacred tool. The short, devotional-like chapters may be used however the reader chooses—because any way that the labyrinth is approached is a right way.

0-8298-1372-1/104 pages/paper/$16.95